TEACHING CURIOUS CHRISTIANS ABOUT JUDAISM

By Deborah J. Levine

Advisor: Sr. Mary Ellen Coombe, nds

Office for Ecumenical and Interreligious Affairs/ Roman Catholic Archdiocese of Chicago IL

Books by Deborah J. Levine

Religious Diversity at Work

Inspire your Inner Global Leader

The Liberator's Daughter

Matrix Model Management System: Guide to Cross Cultural Wisdom

Going Southern: The No-Mess Guide to Success in the South

Deborah J. Levine

TEACHING CURIOUS CHRISTIANS ABOUT JUDAISM

© Deborah J. Levine 2014

Published by Deborah Levine Enterprises, LLC

Chattanooga, TN 37412

1 (888) 451-2798

web: www.americandiversityreport.com

e-mail: info@americandiversityreport.com

Previously published by Liturgy Publications of the Archdiocese of Chicago.

Cover Design: LLPIX Design

Editing and Formatting: BZHercules.com

Foreword

Recently, I was invited to give a workshop to the youth leadership in our Diocese on Ecumenism and Interreligious Dialogue. During that time, I became aware that our young people today are coming into more contact with youth from various religious traditions about which they know very little. As our world becomes smaller and smaller, it is important to understand the religious beliefs of others and how those beliefs motivate their actions.

I am encouraged that a revised edition of *Teaching Christian Children about Judaism* is being issued. I first used it in 1999 when our middle school literature class was reading a novel set in first century (C.E.) Jerusalem and the teacher asked me to come to the class and speak to them about the Jewish practices mentioned in the novel. This book helped to explain in very clear and easy to understand terms the basic beliefs and practices of Judaism. Since then, it has been a valuable resource for me. The glossary in the back is an excellent reference for use with both children and adults.

I appreciate this valuable resource that Ms. Deborah J. Levine has provided in the original book, and now in its revised edition, *Teaching Christian Children about Judaism*. This book can be an aid in helping young people better understand Judaism and in fostering dialogue and mutual respect.

Rev. Msgr. T. Allen Humbrecht

Ecumenical and Interreligious Officer,

Diocese of Knoxville

Acknowledgements

Many thanks for the long-time support and mentoring of my advisor and friend, Sr. Mary Ellen Coombe, nds, Associate Director of the Office for Ecumenical and Interreligious Affairs/ Roman Catholic Archdiocese of Chicago IL.

I greatly appreciate the expertise and helping hand extended by Dr. Amy-Jill Levine, University Professor of New Testament and Jewish Studies, E. Rhodes and Leona B. Carpenter Professor of New Testament Studies, and Professor of Jewish Studies at the Divinity School and College of Arts and Science of Vanderbilt University. Many thanks also to Dr. Stephen R. Haynes, Professor of Religious Studies at Rhodes College, for his valuable feedback.

Much gratitude to Monsigneur Allen Humbrecht, Ecumenical and Interreligious Officer of the Diocese of Knoxville, who asked me to update and reprint this book which he'd been using with children and adult education for more than twenty years. I'm honored that he took the new edition to Vatican City as a gift for Pope Francis.

Table of Contents

Foreword...4

Acknowledgements 5

How to Use this Book and Its Lessons...7

Introduction...11

Lesson 1: The Liturgical Year 14

Lesson 2: The High Holy Days..21

Lesson 3: Hanukkah 27

Lesson 4: Passover 34

Lesson 5: Scripture 42

Lesson 6: Prayer and the Sabbath..49

Lesson 7: Gathering in the Synagogue...55

APPENDIX A: JEWISH SACRED FOOD 63

APPENDIX B: MORE ON HOLIDAYS 66

APPENDIX C: COLORING PAGES 68

APPENDIX D: GLOSSARY..71

About the Author 75

How to Use this Book and Its Lessons

There are seven lessons in this book that can be used consecutively or individually, along with a glossary and a section on food that can be used for general orientation at any time. For older students, the lesson entitled "The Liturgical Year," is a good beginning lesson and can be referred to as a guide in the application of the other lessons. The sections on specific holidays can be coordinated to coincide with the appropriate season. The section on high holidays can be used in the fall along with a lesson on Scripture. The lesson on Hanukkah can be used post-Thanksgiving and into December. The Passover chapter is best suited for the spring season. The lesson on prayer and the Sabbath is applicable throughout the year, as is the lesson on the synagogue, which might be coordinated with a synagogue field trip.

The Lessons

1. The Preparation: Lesson Plan

Background information is included with each lesson. The teacher or leader should read this background material in preparation for the class. They should also read the "Questions and Answers" section before presenting the material in class. This section of "Frequently Asked Questions," along with suggested answers, provides additional familiarity with the background information and allows for more productive discussion.

2. The Lesson Plan

Each lesson has a suggested outline for presenting the material. The suggestions are primarily for interactive, discussion purposes. There will also be discussion ideas for future lesson plans should you wish to go further into depth. In many cases, the lesson plan will contain resources beyond the background information for use in the classroom.

3. The Questions and Answers

The Q&A page contains between six and fourteen common questions that focus on that lesson's topic. These questions, and the answers that are provided, were the results of extensive field-testing. While the field-testing was done in a Catholic parochial school, the questions and answers are applicable to a wide audience. Familiarity with expected questions, along with appropriate answers given in actual classroom settings, will provide a helpful comfort level to teachers, leaders, and trainers using this book.

4. The Takeaway Page

Each lesson includes a Takeaway page that can be provided separately to the students for their individual use. On some Takeaway pages, there are Hebrew words and phrases. "Beloved Hebrew Letters" is an English transliteration that provides the approximate sound of the Hebrew. Practice with the transliteration in class to give the students some experience with the sound of Hebrew language. The student can then practice the Hebrew at home using the Takeaway page. Complementing the Takeaway page is a summary page with a brief synopsis of the lesson. For young students, this page can be shared with parents and family to achieve a better understanding of that lesson. For older students, the summary can be part of the Takeaway page as a study guide of the major elements in that lesson.

Introducing a Lesson

Many students have had minimal exposure to Judaism and little reason to study it. The teacher or leader will need to prepare the students for the material by establishing a context for the lesson. The lessons in this book can be taught by a Christian teacher in the absence of a representative of the Jewish community. However, this book was designed for optimal use in a team setting, where it should be a Christian team member who would make the introduction to lesson, and the Jewish team member would teach the background material and field questions about Judaism. The Christian team member would begin the lesson with a personal introduction, followed by an introduction of it for her Jewish counterpart.

Knowing that it is often not possible to have a teaching team for these lessons, the remainder of this book will be geared to the individual Christian teacher, leader, or trainer. Christian teachers can augment the introduction, in the absence of a Jewish team member, by discussing their personal interest in studying Judaism. Alternately, they can refer to the following material.

What does "Jewish" mean?

We cannot assume that our students understand the connection between today's Jewish people and Judaism as a religion. Not all of our students, particularly the young ones, will have had the opportunity to meet Jewish people. Therefore, establishing a context for learning about Judaism requires building on a recognizable common denominator. That denominator is most likely to be scripture. However, while Christians may refer to the Old Testament, this is not terminology used in Judaism. Jews may use the term "Hebrew Scriptures," although it is not an exact equivalent of Old Testament. Torah can refer to the Hebrew Scriptures in general, but is technically a term for the first five books of the Torah known as the "Five Books of Moses," or The Pentateuch. In addition to scripture, Judaism has centuries of rabbinic law and commentary on the Torah that defines how Judaism is observed today.

A good strategy for creating awareness of the distinctiveness of the Judaism and Christianity is to discuss the Jewish people in scripture. Divide a list of biblical names into "Jewish People in the Old Testament" and "Jewish People in the New Testament." The lists will help define the formative stories of both Judaism and Christianity for our curious Christians.

Judaism centers around the story of Creation, the Exodus, and the Promised Land. Christianity centers on the story of Jesus, his teachings, and the life of the early Church. Refer to these lists when speaking of traditions and rituals that pertain to either the Jewish story or the Christian story.

Jewish people in the Old Testament: **Jewish people in the New Testament:**

Jewish people in the Old Testament:	Jewish people in the New Testament:
Abraham	Elizabeth
David	Jesus
Deborah	John the Baptist
Isaac	Joseph
Jacob	Paul
Jonah	Mark
Joshua	Martha
Judah	Mary
Leah	Matthew
Miriam	Peter
Moses	The Apostles
Noah	
Rachel	
Rebecca	
Ruth	
Samuel	
Sarah	
Solomon	
The 12 Tribes	
The Prophets	

Throughout the lessons, you will notice the students working to understand the differences between Christianity and Judaism. Initially, the students will work to understand that Judaism and Christianity are different religions. Younger Christian students are just beginning to identify with their own tradition and often find it difficult to make the connection that, for example, Jews do not celebrate Christmas or Easter. It can be helpful to return to the names and the stories in both the Old and New Testaments, defining for the students the formative stories of Judaism and Christianity. It will become clear how central the story of Passover is to Judaism, as are the stories of Christmas and Easter to

Christianity. The traditions and rituals of these holy days can then be separated and gain a context in the religious community from which they evolved. Using the vocabulary of "root stories" is a helpful tool in establishing the distinctive religious identities.

Who are Jews today?

The next step is to establish a connection with contemporary Jews. Explain that Jews today are descendants of the tribes of Judah or Levi. Also, there are no Israelites today, only Israelis and the modern state of Israel.

Ask the students if they know Jewish people. Teachers should note that the field-testing of this manual has shown that some children in parochial schools have Jewish relatives in their family. Students of any age may have Jewish neighbors, friends, and colleagues. If no one in the class has connections to Jewish people, the teacher may wish to draw on television shows and movies depicting Jewish characters.

Why should we learn about Judaism and Jewish people? Why does the Church ask us to do this?

1. They are friends, neighbors, and sometimes relatives.

2. The Jewish community has suffered from the prejudice of others.

3. The task of education is to break down stereotypes and foster understanding.

4. Jesus and many of his followers were Jewish.

5. Learning about Judaism promotes a better understanding of Christianity.

6. The Old Testament is the story of the Jewish people.

Now that we have established a context, the teacher and students are ready to explore Judaism and its meaning in Christianity. For young children, teachers should read the chapter aloud and then ask for questions. The Q & A provided in the book can prompt and augment the students' curiosity. The coloring pages at the back of the book can complement the lessons with hands-on learning. Older students can take turns reading the chapters aloud. They can discuss each question and write their own answers in essays and exams.

Introduction

Deborah Levine, Coordinator of the National Workshop on Christian-Jewish Relations, and the late Joseph Cardinal Bernadin of the Archdiocese of Chicago

It is impossible to understand Christianity without reference to Judaism. The two are inextricably linked. Consider the following:

1. The early followers of Jesus were Jews.

2. Jews and Christians share some common scriptures.

3. Judaism is the source of the Christian proclamation that God is one and that God is merciful, gracious, and in a covenantal relationship with humankind.

4. Jesus was a Jew, and his words and deeds cannot be fully understood apart from an understanding of the first-century Jewish life.

5. Christian worship, especially the Eucharist, finds its roots in Jewish liturgical life.

The relationship has grown, as noted in the *National Catholic Register* (Peter Jesserer Smith, 11/8/2013). "Blessed Pope John XXIII reset Catholic-Jewish relations in the 1960s, seeking to reconcile the grievances of the past, in which Catholics had treated Jews less like beloved brothers and more like strangers — or worse, as enemies. The Catholic Church approved that outreach in 1965 at the Second Vatican Council with the document *Nostra Aetate*, and Popes Paul VI, Blessed John Paul II, and Benedict XVI all continued efforts to deepen those relations ... But Pope Francis' pontificate represents a new chapter of deeper understanding and friendship between Jews and Catholics."

Yes, the relationship between Jews and Christians throughout history has been a troubled one. In the first century, Christianity was moving away from Judaism, but the "parting of ways" took place gradually. It was not until the middle of the Fourth Century that Christianity and Judaism were distinct religions and, even then, Jewish Jesus-worshipers may not have stopped considering themselves Jews for another century. However, before this complete separation, many of the New Testament and patristic polemics against Jews and Judaism were composed and circulated. These polemics reflected the confrontations between the emerging church and the developing rabbinic tradition, both of which were concerned with issues of group identity and appropriate lines of demarcation.

Beginning in the 11th Century, the Crusaders perpetrated violent acts against the Jewish communities of Christian Europe. During the following centuries, in consolidating its secular power, the Church was ambivalent in its policies towards the Jews. On the one hand, it sought to suppress the attractiveness of Judaism to potential converts. On the other hand, it desired to protect the existence of Judaism as a witness to the validity of the Scriptures of Israel, upon which Christian proclamation is based. The teachings of contempt against Jews and Judaism, initially only theoretical, became concrete in such tragic acts against Jews as forced exile, forced baptism, Talmud burnings, blood libels, and consignment to ghettos. Beginning in the 10th Century, the Crusaders perpetrated violent acts against the Jewish communities of Christian Europe, despite the opposition of the Pope. By the end of the 16th Century, the Jewish communities of Western Europe were decimated.

From the Enlightenment until World War II, Jews were gradually freed from the ghettos and many contributed significantly to European culture and society. However, much of European society still considered Jews to be "outsiders." During this time, a pseudoscientific racism developed and Nazism carried this theory to its most extreme to justify the Holocaust, in which, ultimately, two-thirds of the Jews in Europe were systematically murdered.

This shock of this event and the ensuing understanding of what had happened began with the liberation of the Nazi death camps by the Allied Armies. Gradually, a "Never Again" mentality produced a determination for change and a hopeful outlook for both Christians and Jews. On a personal note, my father was one of the liberators in the Allied Army in the

American military who opened one of these death camps. I feel compelled to write this book, not only to heal wounds, but to help improve understanding and relationships going forward. As my father would say, "I live in hope."

That spirit of hope for the future grew within the Catholic Church, bearing fruit in *Nostra Aetate*, the second Vatican Council's declaration on the relation of Catholicism to non-Christian religions. For almost 2000 years, the dominant understanding of the relationship between Christianity and Judaism was that Judaism had been supplanted by Christianity. Judaism represented the old covenant, and Christianity represented the new. Judaism's rule of law was contrasted with the sovereignty of love preached by Jesus, a view that argued that the church had made Judaism obsolete, unnecessary.

Nostra Aetate pointed the way for a new approach. It used the imagery of St. Paul in Romans 11 to say that Christianity is grafted onto the Tree of Salvation whose trunk may be interpreted as Judaism. This implies a continuing life for Judaism, for if the trunk has died, the branches can hardly remain healthy. *Nostra Aetate* also put to rest the false teaching that the Jewish people are eternally guilty for the crime of killing Jesus, a crime referred to as "Christ-killer" and later heard as "deicide." This false notion has been responsible for the persecution of many Jews throughout history. The final section of *Nostra Aetate* also repudiates anti-Semitism as incompatible with the gospel.

Since 1965, there have been significant changes in liturgy and in education materials. This activity has helped the church not only to realize that the recovery of the spirit and teachings of biblical Judaism is vital for a healthy Christianity, but also to recognize Judaism as an ongoing, vigorous tradition that stands independent of Christianity. The next step was to create the materials to integrate these teachings into the everyday life of the Church and provide Christian adults and children with an experience of the life of Judaism.

This book, originally published in the mid-1990s, received the National Catholic Press Association award. Its goal was to provide education on many levels with an emphasis on the experiential, not just on the intellectual component, of learning. Originally, the book was primarily geared to the education of young students and had the title *Teaching Christian Children about Judaism.* However, over the years, its lessons were used not only in grades one through eight, the intended audience, but in high schools, adult learning, and professional training. Revised and republished almost two decades later, the lessons have been revised for more universal application and useful material added, particularly the "Tips on Food." The book's title now represents the broad audience it has had, and no doubt will continue to have, *Teaching Curious Christians about Judaism.*

Lesson 1: The Liturgical Year

Introduction

Liturgical year tells the story of a religious community. Religious festivals, celebrations, and commemorations define the community's sacred space, time, and history. Judaism has been a model for many religions, including Christianity, on how to create and affirm the religious life of the community to the use of a liturgical calendar. By studying the Jewish calendar, Christians can better understand the development of their own liturgical calendar and its role in shaping their faith, as well as gaining an appreciation and understanding of the Jewish community.

Background

The first five books of the Torah, or Pentateuch, are read from beginning to end each year. Its ancient stories contain the keys to understanding the Jewish concept of days, weeks, and seasons. *Genesis* begins with God creating the world in six days, resting on the seventh. The story defines the week as having seven days, the seventh being the Sabbath. The day begins at sundown so that God's miracle of creating light from darkness is appreciated every day of the week. It means that Jewish holidays, including the Sabbath, begin when the sun goes down and end also at sunset.

Jews use the abbreviations B.C.E. (Before the Common Era) and C.E. (Common or Christian Era) rather than B.C. (Before Christ) and A.D. (Anno Domini: in the year of the Lord) The Jewish calendar is dated from the time of creation, as calculated by Jews from the Bible. Therefore, 2016-2017 is the year 5777 in the Jewish calendar which largely lunar, unlike our solar civic calendar. The months in the Jewish calendar are measured by the moon and are therefore shorter than our secular months, having only 28 days. Therefore, Jewish months do not coincide exactly with the dates of our secular months. Nor is the leap year calculated as we do it today. An extra month is added to the calendar seven times within a 19-year period, making a solar adjustment that keeps holidays generally anchored in a specific season. In our secular calendar, we make that adjustment by adding a day into February every four years.

The ancient Jewish community was one of farmers and shepherds. Their agricultural-based customs are reflected in the three major harvest festivals: Passover, or *Pesach*, comes in the spring; Shavuot comes in the summer; and Sukkot comes in the fall. These holidays once included pilgrimages during which a portion of the harvest was offered to God at the Temple in Jerusalem. Since the Temple was destroyed centuries ago, the harvest pilgrimage rituals have been adapted for celebration in the home and in the synagogue.

In addition to having seasonal themes, Jewish holidays also have biblical and religious themes. Sukkot comes in the fall and is linked to Thanksgiving for the bounty of the field. Members of the community, and sometimes individual families, would build *sukkah* in which they gather, study, and eat during the holiday. A *sukkah* is a temporary dwelling, a hut or booth with four sides and slots for roof that permit a view of the stars. The *sukkah* is decorated with vegetables, fruit, paper chains, and pictures of Jerusalem. Historically, farmers would live in these booths for days during the harvest. Sukkot is a time of joyous thanksgiving for the harvest, especially before winter sets in. It is a time of great abundance and celebration.

Passover celebrates joy in new life with the spring harvest. The egg and parsley of the Passover Seder meal celebration is a seasonal representation of new life. Passover is linked to the story of *Exodus* and recounts the history of the Jewish people's Exodus from Egypt and entrance into the Promised Land. This event is a central element of the holiday. Passover highlights the core beliefs of Judaism, including religious freedom. (See Lesson Four for more information on Passover.) Forty-nine days from the second night of Passover is the harvest holiday called Shavuot. In addition to being a harvest celebration, Shavuot commemorates the historic event of Moses receiving the Ten Commandments at Mount Sinai. Religiously, the celebration of Shavuot includes studying the Torah and honoring religious education.

The Jewish year begins with a communal gathering at the new year, Rosh HaShanah, which comes in the fall season. The beginning of a new year marks ten days of solemn reflection by the Jewish community and humanity's place in God's creation. The traditions and laws of the Torah and the centuries of rabbinic commentary on the Torah are beloved and revered for the ways they shape Jewish identity and allow the Jewish community to honor God. As the Christian liturgical year links Christians with Jesus, the Jewish holy days link the Jewish people to the Torah, their history, and their covenant with God.

Lesson Plan

1. Begin this lesson with how liturgical calendars celebrate our stories by discussing major Christian holy days throughout the year. Focus on Easter, including Good Friday, as well as Christmas. Concentrate on how these holidays illuminate the life of Jesus and participation in that life.

2. Discuss how the days and weeks are structured in the story of *Genesis*. Talk about the Jewish Sabbath and when it begins and ends. Read out loud the background information about how Jewish holidays observe seasonal, historical, and religious themes.

3. Talk about what life is like in an agricultural society. How would the Israelites have harvested their crops in biblical times? What would it be like to celebrate the harvest in a *sukkah*? Invite a member of the Jewish community to share their stories about celebrating Sukkot today.

4. Examine a Jewish calendar together, comparing it with our secular calendar. Note that the names of the months are different from the months we know. The Jewish months are: Nisan, Iyar, Sivan, Tammuz, Av, Elul, Tishri, Heshvan, Kislev, Tevet, Shevat, Elul, Adar, and Adar 2 (in leap years).

5. Explain that the Jewish year is counted from the beginning of creation more than 5000 years ago. Have your students research today's date according to the Jewish calendar. For example, Wednesday, January 1, 2014 was, according to the Jewish calendar, the 29th day of the month of Tevet in the year 5774.

Q&A

1. Why do the Jewish people celebrate Sukkot in a sukkah?

The process of building the sukkah booth with wood and branches (no nails!) not only recreates biblical times, but creates a link between then and now that is timeless. For the seven or eight days (traditions vary) of Sukkot, Jews of all ages and in every locale, eat, study, and pray as their ancestors did, erasing the centuries between the countless generations.

2. How does Sukkot relate to the American celebration of Thanksgiving?

Sukkot is a harvest celebration giving thanks not only for an abundant harvest, but for a harvest in the Promised Land. When the pilgrims came to North America, they also gave thanks to God for the harvest. While Thanksgiving didn't become a national holiday until centuries later, Thanksgiving was a long-held tradition.

3. Why is it so important for the Jewish people to honor religious education during a holiday?

The gift of the Ten Commandments, which appear twice in the Torah, in the books of *Exodus* and *Deuteronomy*, is celebrated on Shavuot. Shavuot is celebrated by the study of Torah as a whole. Study of the Torah, and the generations of rabbinic commentary on it, is central to Jewish education. The religious and ethical obligations embedded in the biblical stories shape the lives of the community and its individuals.

4. Why do Jewish holidays come at different times each year?

The Jewish holidays actually do occur at the same time every year, according to the Jewish calendar. However, given the nature of a lunar calendar, the holidays appear to be on different days, weeks, and even months every year. This appearance is heightened by the fact that they do swing back and forth from the beginning to the end of the season, given the nature of the adjustment to what we call the leap year. However, the holidays are firmly in place on specific days, during a specific month of the Jewish year.

5. Why isn't the Jewish Sabbath on Sunday?

Historically, the Sabbath fell on Saturday, beginning Friday night and ending Saturday at sundown. Christianity eventually moved its Sabbath to Sunday, differentiating itself from the Jewish Sabbath and from the Jewish tradition of beginning the Sabbath at sundown the previous day. Note that some Christian groups, particularly the Seventh-day Adventists, continue to observe the Jewish Sabbath timeframe.

6. Why don't you ever see AD after Jewish dates?

Anno Domini means in the "Year of Our Lord" in Latin and is abbreviated as AD. The secular calendar uses the Christian point of reference for its numbering and begins counting with the birth of Jesus as Year One. The Jewish calendar begins with its calculation of creation thousands of years earlier. Therefore, the use of AD is not applicable, and the designation CE is used, meaning Common Era. The designation of BC, meaning Before Christ, is also not applicable to the Jewish calendar. The designation of BCE, meaning Before the Common Era, is often used in its place by the Jewish community as an inclusive term.

TAKEAWAY PAGE

When the Jewish people celebrate their holidays throughout the year, they remember and focus on major ideas. First, they remember the ancient stories of the Jewish people as written in the Bible as their own. Second, they celebrate the season as well as the holiday as part of the gift of God's creation.

Here is a list of major Jewish holidays:

Shabbat

The weekly day of prayer and rest, celebrated from sunset Friday to sunset Saturday.

Rosh HaShanah

The Jewish New Year that begins the Ten Days of Awe and Reflection

Yom Kippur

The holiest day in the Jewish year after the Sabbath. It is a day of prayer, fasting, and communal atonement and concludes the Ten Days of Awe.

Sukkot

The joyful thanksgiving festival of the fall harvest.

Passover

The springtime harvest celebrating the Exodus of the Israelites from Egypt with the participation at the Passover meal, the Seder, reliving the journey to freedom and the Promised Land.

Shavuot

The summer harvest festival that also commemorates the receiving of the Torah and the Ten Commandments from Moses at Mount Sinai.

Hanukkah

The wintertime celebration of the rededication of the Temple in Jerusalem in biblical times. It is also called the Festival of Lights and is often spelled/translated from the Hebrew as Chanukah.

SUMMARY: THE LITURGICAL YEAR

The liturgical year with its festivals, celebrations, and commemorations, defines the community's sacred space, time, and history. Judaism has been a model for many religions, including Christianity, on creating and affirming the religious life of the community through the use of the liturgical calendar.

The ancient Jewish community was one of farmers and shepherds, and their customs are reflected in the Jewish calendar. There are three major harvest festivals: Passover in the spring, Shavuot in the summer, in Sukkot in the fall. These holidays once included pilgrimages during which a portion of the harvest was offered to God at the Temple in Jerusalem. Since the temple was destroyed centuries ago, the harvest pilgrimage rituals have been adapted for the home and a synagogue.

These seasonal celebrations are also linked to biblical and religious themes. The Torah is read each year from beginning to end and the ancient stories are woven into the seasons of the year and into the historical and religious life of the Jewish community. As the Christian liturgical year links Christmas, Easter, and Jesus to express its root story, the Jewish holy days link the Jewish people to the Exodus, the Promised Land, and the Torah.

Lesson 2: The High Holy Days

Shofar - Ram's Horn

Introduction

Rosh HaShanah, the Jewish New Year (literal translation from the Hebrew is "head of the year"), begins on the evening of the new moon of the new year and is celebrated for two days. These days are part of the Ten Days of Awe that conclude with the Day of Atonement, Yom Kippur. This period of holy days is the most sacred time of the year, other than the weekly Sabbath, and are often the largest gathering of the Jewish community during the year. These ten days, beginning with Rosh HaShanah and concluding with Yom Kippur, are known as the Jewish High Holy Days. They are both festive and solemn, giving thanks for life while acknowledging our finite days.

Background

The Jewish New Year falls on the first two days of the month of Tishri and begins a time of collective contemplation by the community. The distinctly sacred time, and the distinctly Jewish traditions that the community shares worldwide, are designed to bring the Jewish people closer to understanding the Jews' covenant with God, the requirements of that covenant, and the gift of life for yet another year.

As they remember the fragile nature of life, each person must right the wrongs they have committed so that they may be judged as righteous human beings and good Jews. If they were to die tomorrow, would they be judged favorably? Have they obeyed the Ten Commandments and other laws? Have they tried to right the wrongs that they have done to others? During this period, individual Jews apologize directly to the people they have hurt or offended in the past year, acknowledge mistakes in the past, and set expectations for doing better in the coming year.

In ancient times, the new year was announced by the sound of the shofar (ram's horn). The shofar continues to be blown in synagogues all over the world today, calling Jews to prayer and in celebration of the Jewish new year. The shofar is an ancient symbol connected to the hope of messianic redemption. When the Messiah comes, the shofar will announce the resurrection of the dead and call all Jews to prayer in Jerusalem. While Jews do not believe that Jesus was the Messiah, the concept of the Messiah has been a theme in Judaism since biblical times.

Yom Kippur concludes the Ten Days of Awe. On this Day of Atonement, the Jewish community fasts to purify itself and to set apart the experience of repentance from ordinary days. The Jewish congregation shares in the suffering of all those past and present who suffered, appreciating the sacrifices made. The traditional prayer meaning "all vows", *Kol Nidre* is sung by the cantor, who leads the liturgical music in the synagogue. When Yom Kippur comes to an end, the community breaks the fast together and celebrates the opportunity to begin life anew.

The underlying themes of the High Holy Days are repentance, redemption, and the renewal of God's gift of life. These themes remain closely related to the land and the seasons in Judaism and developed differently in Christianity. Yet, the understanding of the gift of life as coming from God and the struggle to be worthy of this gift are vital elements of both religions.

Lesson Plan

1. Have the students talk about the meaning of God's commandments. Discuss Lent as a time of year when Christians ask themselves if they have been living the way God intended. Have the students discuss what Christians do, and should do, during Lent.

2. Discuss what Rosh HaShanah means to the Jewish people and how they celebrate it. Compare the celebration of the Jewish new year with the celebration of the secular new year and include the idea of New Year's resolutions.

3. Listen to the sounds of the Days of Awe. Share one of the many YouTube videos demonstrating the blowing of the shofar. Discuss what it sounds like and how the sounds impact the listener. Share a video of Kol Nidre music and discuss how it sounds.

4. Develop fresh apples and get the slices in honey for a traditional Jewish new year snack. Discuss why the double sweetness of the honey and apple together is a good symbol for beginning a new year.

5. Practice saying Happy New Year in Hebrew - "*L'Shana Tovah.*"

6. Ask students to create a list of the people to whom they might offer an apology for actions in the past year. Have them create a list of resolutions for leading a righteous life in the next year.

Q&A

1. How is the sound of the shofar made?

The shofar can be blown in a loud, long, clear blasts or in short blasts or in staccato ones. The rhythm and sequence is laid out ritualistically. The final blast closing Yom Kippur symbolizes the unity of the community and a sense of completeness.

2. Who blows the shofar?

It is considered an honor and great achievement to blow the shofar in the synagogue. A Jewish adult member of the synagogue is eligible, but it's not easy to blow the shofar, and they will need to practice and demonstrate that they are able to perform.

3. Why do Jews eat apples and honey when they celebrate the new year?

Apples are a symbol of life, knowledge, and abundance. Honey is sweet and a special treat. Together, the apples and honey are a metaphor for a good, sweet life. The use of food to celebrate life is a common theme in Judaism.

4. Why is the Kol Nidre music on the Day of Atonement so sad?

Kol Nidre is a musical lament in which the Jewish people are reminded of the fragility of life. While *Kol Nidre* is part of the ritual renewal of life and the covenant, it is also an acknowledgement of the inevitability of death and the mourning of loved ones.

5. Do Jewish people eat anything during Yom Kippur?

Fasting from food and drink begins at sunset on Yom Kippur and extends to sunset the following day when Yom Kippur ends with a big meal. Children under thirteen and those physically unable to fast for health reasons are exempt from the fasting. (For more information on dietary laws, see the Appendix: Tips on Food).

6. When the Jewish community gathers in the synagogue on the high holy days, they dress up and wear good clothes to start a new year. The clothes are not party apparel, but are often the best clothes they own for a religious celebration. For Yom Kippur, it is the tradition to wear white.

TAKEAWAY PAGE

The shofar is a ram's horn. The sounds of the shofar being blown reinforces the prayers during the High Holy Days.

Rosh HaShanah, the Jewish New Year, is the beginning of the most sacred time of the year for Jewish people. The New Year begins the High Holy Days, a period of celebration, prayer, and atonement lasting for ten Days of Awe, concluding with Yom Kippur.

Here is a new year's greeting in Hebrew

It means "A good new year!" and is pronounced "*Shanah Tovah.*"

SUMMARY – THE HIGH HOLY DAYS

Rosh HaShanah, the Jewish new year, falls on the evening of the new moon of the new year, the first two days of the month of Tishri. It is a solemn occasion as well as a festive one. It begins the Ten Days of Awe, which end with the Day of Atonement, Yom Kippur. Rosh HaShanah and Yom Kippur are also called the Jewish High Holy Days. They are the most sacred time of the Jewish liturgical calendar.

The Jewish community celebrates God's gift of life during this time while striving to make itself worthy of such a gift. The Jewish community and its members honor the fragile nature of life. They must right the wrongs that they have committed in the past year so that they may be judged as righteous humans beings and good Jews. It is a time to apologize to those we have hurt and to resolve to do better in the coming year.

The shofar (ram's horn) is an ancient tradition and the shofar is still blown in synagogues all over the world today. The underlying theme of the high holy days are repentance, redemption, and the renewal of God's gift of life and covenant with the Jewish people. These themes have been part of Judaism since biblical times, when Jews were close to the land and the seasons. They have developed differently in Judaism and in Christianity, but the understanding of the gift of life coming from God and the struggle to be worthy of this gift have remained important elements of both religions.

Lesson 3: Hanukkah

Hanukkah Menorah

Introduction

Many Jewish holidays commemorate events invested with historical and religious meaning. Hanukkah means "dedication," and it commemorates the rededication of the Temple in Jerusalem after its desecration by foreign forces. The celebration also reaffirms the continuing struggle to live by God's commandments and to lead Jewish lives. This lesson on Hanukkah focuses on the menorah, a public symbol of God's presence with the Jewish people.

Background

The story of Hanukkah is the struggle for religious freedom. In 650 BCE, the foreign rulers of the Israelites decreed that pigs, which were taboo, be sacrificed on the Temple altar. The Israelites were forbidden to observe the Sabbath. Inspired by Matthias and led by his son, Judah, a small group of Jews called *Maccabees* (meaning "hammer") rebelled. The Maccabees risked their lives to live according to Jewish law and to prevent this desecration of their sacred temple.

Although the Maccabees won, the Temple in Jerusalem, the Jews' most holy place, was desecrated. The Jews had to clean and repair the temple, and when they were finished, they rededicated it to God by rekindling the menorah, the candelabrum symbolizing the eternal covenant between God and the Jewish people and the continuity of tradition through the generations. However, there was only enough olive oil to fuel the menorah for one night, and it would take eight days to make more oil. The legend of the miracle of Hanukkah says that the one-day supply of oil burned for eight days and nights until more oil could be made. This is why the Hanukkah menorah has eight candles with a special ninth candle to light the others, unlike the seven-branch menorah of the ancient Temple.

There are eight days of Hanukkah corresponding to the legend of the miracle of the oil in the Temple. Foods cooked in oil are traditional, particularly potato pancakes, called *latkes,* and deep-fried doughnuts, called *Sufganiyot* in Hebrew. Today, candles are used instead of oil. On each successive night, the number of candles lit increases by one. Prayers accompany the lighting of the candles.

Hanukkah is celebrated in the home beginning on the 25th day of the Jewish month of Kislev. Officially, Hanukkah is not a major holy day because it isn't mentioned in the Hebrew Scriptures. In addition, the Maccabees' story was resisted by the early rabbis because of its violence. However, in modern times, Hannukah has become a widely celebrated holiday in the Jewish community. Given its proximity to Christmas, Hanukkah has taken on importance in many countries where Christmas has become a popular, and sometimes commercial, holiday.

It is traditional to give small gifts to children on each night of Hanukkah. The party atmosphere is enhanced with songs, food, and games with toys such as a dreidel, a spinning top. While young people today may be more familiar with the Hanukkah song by Saturday Night Live's Adam Sandler, the traditional favorite Hanukkah song is called "The Dreidel Song (I Have a Little Dreidel)."

"I have a little dreidel,

I made it out of clay,

And when it's dry and ready,

The dreidel I will play."

Lesson Plan

1. Read or tell the historical background of Hanukkah and how Hanukkah is celebrated today in Jewish homes.

2. Bring a dreidel to class to show the students. Point out the four sides of the spinning top with each side, showing a different letter in Hebrew. Share how the letters stand for the first word in the phrase *Nes Gadol Haya Sham*, which means "a great miracle happened there." The word dreidel is Yiddish, originally from the German *drehen*, which means "to turn." The Hebrew word for dreidel is *sivivon*, which means "to spin." Listen to the Dreidel song at https://youtu.be/WKreDYVWark .

3. Allow students to spin the dreidel and compete for who can keep the dreidel spinning the longest with one spin. Dreidels are widely available in areas with a substantial Jewish population during Hanukkah. Alternatively, they can easily be ordered online.

4. Draw a menorah as an eight-branch candelabrum with a ninth candle set apart and/or higher than the others. The ninth candle is called the shamus and is used to light the others. Have a contest for who can be the most creative in the design.

5. Enjoy Hanukkah food: make potato pancakes and serve with applesauce.

6. Watch the YouTube video *Latke Recipe* sung by the Maccabeats: https://youtu.be/fg51la8Yayc

Q&A

1. Do you speak Hanukkah?

Young children may know about Jewish people primarily through Hanukkah, as it usually occurs during the holiday season. Many realize that Jewish prayers and songs are not in English, but may identify the different language with the holiday rather than the religion. It can be helpful to explain that the word Hanukkah is Hebrew and means "dedication" in English. The Hebrew letters on the dreidel can be used to demonstrate how Hebrew has a different alphabet than English. Explain that Hebrew is the sacred language of Jewish prayer and worship, as well as the official language of the state of Israel.

2. Do Jewish children get gifts on Hanukkah the way Christian children get gifts on Christmas?

It is the custom for Jewish children to receive a small gift on each of the eight nights of Hanukkah. Many of the gifts are similar to what a Christian child would receive on Christmas: toys, books, and clothing. However, the gifts will be wrapped in Hanukkah wrapping paper, often with the blue and white colors traditionally associated with the Jewish star. There is no Christmas tree under which presents are placed and the presentation of gifts is relatively informal. Sometimes, gifts may be a handful of *gelt*, which are either real coins or chocolate coins covered with gold foil, which could be used to play dreidel games.

3. What is a Jewish star?

The Jewish star, or Shield of David (Mogen David), is a six-point star created by overlaying two triangles. The Jewish star symbolizes the Jewish people and is featured on the flag of Israel in blue on a white background. The blue and white colors of the flag provide the color scheme for Hanukkah gifts, decorations, and cookies.

4. How long do the Hanukkah candles burn?

The candles burn until they are used up, which takes about an hour. In the Jewish tradition out of respect for God, the source of all light, Hanukkah candles are not blown out. Fresh candles are used each night of Hanukkah and the nine-branched Hanukkah menorah is not used during any holiday or celebration other than Hanukkah.

5. Should we give combined Hanukkah-Christmas cards to Jewish people?

As much as we combine Hanukkah and Christmas to emphasize the diversity of season, it is not advised to combine the two holidays into a single greeting card. Entertaining as some of these cards may be, there is a strong possibility that the Jewish recipient will find it uncomfortable.

6. Should we invite Jewish people to our Christmas party?

The dilemma of parties during December is complex, particularly in schools, organizations, and workplaces that have not only a diverse group of participants, but also have a tradition of celebrating Christmas. While it is appropriate to invite everyone to a Christmas party, it is not appropriate to require attendance. Some groups organize holiday parties during this season to be more inclusive. However, be aware that a holiday party can also be challenging, particularly concerning symbols that Christians may feel are secular, but are perceived by Jewish people to be Christian and religious. Such symbols may include Santa Claus, a Christmas tree, and a red and green color scheme.

TAKEAWAY PAGE

The story of Hanukkah is the story of the struggle for religious freedom, freedom to be Jewish and to practice the Jewish religion. In ancient times, the Maccabees risked their lives to secure the fate of the Jewish people and their Temple. While they won the battle, the Temple was left in ruins. After cleaning and repairing the Temple, the Jewish people found that there was only enough oil for the menorah to burn for one day. The great miracle of Hanukkah is that the oil lasted for the eight days needed to make more oil. Here are the English translations of the prayers over the Hanukkah candles. Notice that Jewish prayers often contain the words bless, blessed, and blessings, a tradition that Christians came to share.

Barukh atah Adonai, Eloheinu, melekh ha'olam, asher kidishanu b'mitz'votav v'tzivanu l'had'lik neir shel Chanukah. (Amen)

1. Blessed are you, Lord our God, King of the universe,

who sanctified us with the Commandments

and commanded us to light the Hanukkah lights.

Barukh atah Adonai, Eloheinu, melekh ha'olam, she'asah nisim la'avoteinu bayamim haheim baziman hazeh. (Amen)

2. Blessed are you, Lord our God, King of the Universe,

who performed miracles for our ancestors in days gone by,

at this season of the year.

(The *Shehecheyanu* blessing is recited only at the start of a holiday, and on special occasions.)

Barukh atah Adonai, Eloheinu, melekh ha'olam, shehecheyanu v'kiyimanu v'higi'anu laz'man hazeh. (Amen)

3. Blessed are You, Lord our God, Ruler of the Universe,

who has granted us life, sustained us

and enabled us to reach this occasion.

SUMMARY - HANUKKAH

Many Jewish holidays commemorate events invested with historical and religious meaning. The story of Hanukkah is the struggle for religious freedom. More than a thousand years ago, the foreign rulers of the Israelites decreed that the Jews were forbidden to observe the Sabbath and used the Temple altar to sacrifice pigs which was taboo. Inspired by Mattathias and led by his son Judah, a small group of Jews called Maccabees (meaning "hammer") rebelled. The Maccabees risked their lives to live as Jews and to prevent the desecration of their sacred Temple.

Although the Maccabees won their battles, the Temple in Jerusalem, the Jews' most holy place, was desecrated. After cleaning and repairs, the temple was rededicated to God by lighting the *menorah*, the candelabrum symbolizing the terminal covenant between God and the Jewish people. The flame was intended to burn continuously, but there was only enough olive oil to fuel the menorah for one night. The legend of the miracle of Hanukkah says that the one-day supply, which was all that was left, lasted for the eight days needed to produce more oil.

Usually celebrated in the home, the Hanukkah holiday begins on the 25th day of the Jewish month of Kislev. For some Jews, Hanukkah is not a major religious holiday. However, for many Jews, particularly those in America where the holiday season has secular and commercial elements as well as religious ones, Hanukkah has become a publicly visible part of the Jewish calendar. The celebration of Hanukkah with songs, gifts, dreidel games, food and candy, gives the holiday a party-like atmosphere that fits well into the holiday season. However, keep in mind that the religious celebration of the holiday, the lighting of the candles with accompanying prayers, is at the heart of the festivities.

Lesson 4: Passover

Passover Seder plate with symbolic food, wine, and matzoh

Introduction

Passover (Pesach) is one of the greatest stories of religious freedom ever told. The Jewish people have commemorated the story of the Exodus for hundreds of generations. Passover retells the story, reliving the Exodus, the Israelites' struggle from slavery to freedom and their covenant with God at Mount Sinai. The quest for religious freedom, for the opportunity to be Jewish freely, has been an ongoing struggle, and the Jewish people commit themselves anew to this goal each Passover.

Passover and Easter occur at roughly the same time every spring. Some of the rituals and symbols of the two celebrations overlap: the Seder table with its symbols of the egg, the wine, and the wafer-like matzoh resonate in both religions. The Jewish heritage of Jesus is especially apparent at this time. The Easter and Passover time of celebration has also been associated historically with conflict and major challenges between Jews and Christians. There have been times when the "deicide" charge was leveled at Jews, holding them forever responsible for the crucifixion of Jesus. In addition, legends grew up suggesting that Jews killed Christians at Passover and used their blood to make the Passover matzoh.

At the Second Vatican Council in 1965, the Catholic Church officially repudiated the centuries-old "deicide" charge and the "blood libel" legends. The document that came out of Vatican II, Nostra Aetate, emphasized God's continuing love for the Jewish people and the ongoing validity of God's covenant with them. Passover and Easter are good opportunities for continuing the respectful dialogue between Christians and Jews.

Background

Passover is traditionally an eight-day celebration (seven days in Israel and Reform Judaism). It is one of the three harvest/pilgrimage festivals in the Jewish calendar and the most prominent of them. Passover is a celebration of spring, after winter, and a celebration of the story of the Exodus. It is a home-based holiday, celebrated with family and friends, with everyone present participating in the experience.

Preparation for Passover is extensive, including a massive spring cleaning and removing leavened food from the home. The Passover Seder is held on the first night of the holiday and is repeated on the second night in more traditional homes. At the Seder, the story of the Exodus is retold, reading from a book called the *Haggadah*. By reading the story, the participants become part of it, as if they too were Israelite slaves in Egypt, struggling for freedom and deliverance.

The story begins with a Pharaoh, the Egyptian king, who forgets that Joseph (of the coat of many colors) and his Jewish cohorts had helped the Egyptians through a major famine. This Pharaoh fears the growing number of Jews in Egypt and orders the murder of Jewish male babies and the enslavement of all Jews. The baby Moses is placed in a basket by his mother and hidden among the reeds by the Nile River. His sister, Miriam, watches over him. The story tells us that Moses is later found and raised by an Egyptian princess.

As an adult, Moses was chosen by God to speak to the Egyptian Pharaoh on behalf of the Israelites. God sends plagues on the Egyptians until they agreed to let the Jews go. The last and most famous of the ten plagues is the death of the firstborn male. Jewish homes, marked by the blood of the lamb, were spared and the Israelites walked through the Red Sea, parted by Moses, to freedom. The forty years of wandering in the desert, God's gift of manna to eat, and the gift of the Ten Commandments at Mount Sinai are all central to the Exodus story and provide the basis for a Jewish community dedicated to justice and piety.

The Passover Seder is a combination of ritual, tradition, prayer, and celebratory meal. The *Haggadah* guides celebrants through the liturgy, often in question and answer format. It is read aloud; sometimes the participants read in unison and often, each person at the Seder table takes a turn in the reading. The *Haggadah* explains the meaning of the different rituals of the service and also of the symbols and ritual foods on the Seder table, including why there is no leavening in Passover food, symbolizing the haste with which the Israelites left Egypt. The Seder participants taste each of the symbolic foods in the order outlined by the *Haggadah*. A ritual Seder plate displays them on the table for all to see: bitter herbs, usually horseradish, to symbolize the bitterness of slavery; boiled eggs and parsley dipped in salt water to symbolize the green life of spring and the tears of the slaves; *charoses* (chopped apples, nuts, cinnamon, and wine) to symbolize the mortar for the bricks the slaves made; the shank bone of a lamb to symbolize the lambs' blood the Jews used to mark their houses when the Angel of Death passed over to take the Egyptian first-born sons.

A favorite part of the Seder is the "Four Questions" usually asked by the youngest person at the table and answered by the oldest: the parent or the adult who is serving as the coordinator of the rituals. The questions follow the introductory question, "Why is this night different from all other nights?" The answers are read from the *Haggadah* and are the same every year. Yet, the ritual engages the young and the old, the host and the guest, as well as relatives, friends, and strangers, no matter how many times they have, or have not attended a Seder. Further, regardless of their connection to the state of Israel, the participants conclude the Seder, as Jews have for centuries, expressing their hope to celebrate Passover "next year in Jerusalem." As the story of the Torah ends within sight of the Promised Land, so does the celebration of Passover.

Lesson Plan

1. Read the story of *Exodus* aloud either from the Hebrew Scriptures or from a *Haggadah*. If the students are old enough to read, let them take turns reading with you. For younger children, let them talk about what it would be like to be the Pharaoh, to be Miriam, or to be Moses.

2. Have the students make a list of the traditional foods on the Seder plate. Ask them to describe how the foods relate to the *Exodus* story.

3. Discuss what it would mean to a small child to recite the first of the four questions in public for the first time.

4. Taste some Passover foods. *Matzoh* can be bought in many supermarkets, as can jars of horseradish for the bitter herbs (white horseradish, if possible). *Charoses* can be made by mixing finely chopped nuts (pecans or walnuts) with chopped apples, grape juice, and cinnamon. Make a sandwich with two small pieces of *matzoh*, putting the *charoses* and bitter herbs between them. This is called a "Hillel" sandwich, named after a famous rabbi and scholar who lived centuries ago.

5. Learn to say the Hebrew word *dayenu*, which means "it would have been enough." The saying refers to each of the wonderful things that God did for the Jewish people in the *Exodus* story. It is also the title and chorus of the well-known Jewish song for Passover.

6. Make a list of all the foods in your house that contain some leavening. Discuss what it would be like to remove all those foods for at least eight days.

Q&A

1. Who goes to a Seder?

The Seder is a family meal. Invitations are often given to friends, neighbors, and Jews without family in the area. Invitations are sometimes extended to non-Jews with an interest in experiencing the Seder.

2. Why is food so important during Passover?

The dietary laws associated with Passover are part of the commemoration of God's delivering the Jewish people from slavery. The ban on leavened food is observed only during the Passover celebration and at no other time during the year. Expressing the story through food is common with Jewish holidays. By sharing the food of the Seder table, and at the same time sharing the *Exodus* story from the *Haggadah*, today's Jewish people are connected to a people that transcends time and place.

3. Are children forced to eat all of the Passover food?

Everyone is encouraged to taste everything. However, no one is pressured to do so, particularly children under thirteen who are not yet considered adults. The foods are not processed for baby formula or baby food. What happens if you get tired of matzoh? Matzoh is not just unleavened bread, but also is also ground up into matzo meal. For variety, the matzo meal can be made into dumplings for soup, stuffing, pancakes, and flourless desserts.

4. How old is the youngest child who asks the Four Questions?

The Four Questions are chanted in Hebrew so that the child who does this part of the Seder must be old enough to learn how to do this. There is no set age, but often elementary school age children have already learned to chant these questions in Hebrew.

5. Why do some people have grape juice instead of wine at the Seder?

The Seder participants are required to fill their wine glasses four times during the meal. However, most Seder tables have grape juice made especially for Passover for young children and those who are ill or unable to tolerate the wine.

6. Where do people sit for the Seder?

Participants are seated at the dining room table, and often, extra tables are set up to accommodate large crowds. Pillows from around the house of various sizes are put on the chairs so that people can lean on them. In ancient days, chairs and pillows were luxuries that slaves could not afford. The Seder marks freedom by inserting these luxuries into the rituals observed today.

7. What are the doorposts referred to in the story of the lambs' blood marking the Jewish houses?

The doorposts are the entranceway to the house. This entrance has had strong symbolic meaning for the Jewish community. Contemporary Jewish homes often have a religious object (mezuzah) on its doorposts to remind those who pass through the entrance of God's teachings.

TAKEAWAY PAGE

At Passover, the Jewish community retells and relives the story of the *Exodus*. Passover is celebrated with a Seder meal while reading the *Haggadah,* the guide through the rituals, the *Exodus* story, prayers, and songs as well as the Four Questions that explain the holiday.

The Four Questions: *Ma Nishtanah* (What is different?)

Introduction: Why is this night different from all other nights?

Ma nishtanah halailah hazeh mikol haleilot?

מַה נִּשְׁתַּנָּה הַלַּיְלָה הַזֶּה מִכָּל הַלֵּילוֹת?

1. Why is it that on all other nights we eat leavened products and matzoh, and on this night only matzoh?

We eat only matzoh because our ancestors could not wait for their breads to rise when they were fleeing slavery in Egypt, and so they were flat when they came out of the oven.

2. Why is it that on all other nights we eat all vegetables, and on this night, only bitter herbs?

We eat only *maror,* a bitter herb, to remind us of the bitterness of slavery that our ancestors endured while in Egypt.

3. Why is it that on all other nights we don't dip our food even once, and on this night, we dip twice?

The first dip, green vegetables in salt water, symbolizes the replacing of our tears with gratitude, and the second dip, *maror* in *charoses*, symbolizes the sweetening of our burden of bitterness and suffering.

4. Why is it that on all other nights, we eat sitting or reclining, and on this night, we only recline?

We recline at the Seder table because in ancient times, a person who reclined at a meal was a free person, while slaves and servants stood.

SUMMARY - PASSOVER

Passover is an eight-day celebration (seven days when in Israel) of one of the best-known stories of religious freedom ever told. Passover is the holiday of the spring harvest, but also relives the Exodus, the Israelites' struggle from slavery to freedom and their covenant with God at Mount Sinai. The quest for religious freedom, the right to be Jewish freely, is an ongoing struggle, and the Jewish people commit themselves anew to it each Passover holiday.

Passover is a family event, celebrated in the home with every member and guest taking part. Considerable preparation, including removing leavened food from the home, sets apart the time and place for observing Passover as sacred. Starting on the first night of Passover, the story of the Exodus is experienced, not just retold, at the Seder meal. This Seder combines ritual, liturgy, tradition, prayer, and celebration. The *Haggadah* book guides the celebrants through the Seder liturgy, which has been passed down through generations.

For centuries, Jews all over the world have concluded the Seder by saying, "Next year in Jerusalem." Jerusalem symbolizes Israel, the land of the covenant with God. The desire to return to this land has included the desire to practice Judaism without restriction. Passover is often seen as a holiday honoring the struggle for religious freedom for all people.

Lesson 5: Scripture

The Torah scroll is read using a pointer or "Yad" (Hebrew, meaning "hand")

Introduction

The Old Testament of Christianity is known as TaNaKh in the Jewish community. This word is comprised of the Hebrew initials for Scripture's thirty-nine books in three sections: Torah, Prophets, and Writings. The term "Torah" can be applied to all three sections, or to the Five Books of Moses. These Books, also known as "The Pentateuch" include: Genesis, Exodus, Leviticus, Numbers, and Deuteronomy. They are the key to understanding the covenant between God and the Jewish people. Torah study is embedded in Jewish worship and can be widely interpreted to include centuries of rabbinic commentary (Talmud) on Scripture and its meaning. As God's gift to the Jewish people, the words of the Torah are divinely inspired and the Torah scroll is a sacred object.

After the destruction of the Temple by the Romans in 70 CE, there followed centuries of commentary and debate (Talmud) by rabbis, the teachers who replaced the Temple priests as community and religious leaders, on Scripture and its meaning. The Talmudic writings are comprised of its core Scripture commentary and code of law, the *Mishnah,* and ongoing debate between rabbis, the *Gemarah.* The Talmud provides for both the transmission of tradition and for the ability to shape tradition for the Jewish community in many lands and through countless generations.

Background

The Torah scrolls are handwritten in Hebrew on sheets of parchment, paper made from the hide of a kosher animal, typically the back of a calf, that are sewn together. Some scrolls are kept in special cases, but many are wound around two wooden poles. The Torah scroll is cherished for its history, religious significance, and artistry. Each scroll is written in black ink by a scribe who is professionally trained. The scribe copies from an older scroll to make sure there are no mistakes. There can be some variation in the shape of Hebrew letters according to three major cultural origins, but the words are identical, handing down the Torah intact. The writing is checked before each sheet of parchment is sewn together to complete the scroll. Most of the scribes who write the scrolls are in Israel, while scribes who check their work are located around the world. A computer is often used to ensure accuracy. Some mistakes can be changed using a pumice stone to erase letters. Mistakes in the words for "God" cannot be corrected; those sheets must be disposed of respectfully.

The Torah scroll is "dressed" in a heavy decorative covering for its protection and beautification. The poles are often adorned with bells, whose sound is associated with the rituals surrounding the reading of the Torah. An engraved silver disk, or "breastplate," is hung on the Torah, symbolic of the ancient priesthood in the Temple of Jerusalem. Sacred and historic, Torah scrolls are kept in the Ark of the Covenant, a structure that is central to the sanctuary of the synagogue.

After taking the Torah from the Ark, a procession carrying the Torah is made through the aisles of the congregation. The congregants may touch it with their prayer book (*siddur*) or the fringes (*tzitzit)* of their prayer shawls, then kiss the *siddur* or *tzitzit.* It is an honor to hold, touch, and read from the Torah. Readers, who must be thirteen years of age or older, are called to the Torah using their Hebrew names by the rabbi leading the worship service. In order to maintain the scrolls, a pointer (*yad*, meaning "hand" in Hebrew) is used by readers so that their fingers do not touch the parchment. The Hebrew of the Torah does not contain vowels, so the readers must know the portion in advance, and are often able to chant the verses in the ancient melodies still taught today.

The word "God" is not used when translating the Hebrew prayers into Hebrew. Rather, there are descriptive phrases and labels in Hebrew such as King of the Universe, Ruler of the World, and the Creator. God's true name is unknowable and so powerful that it should not be said aloud. Some Jews will refer to God simply as "The Name" in Hebrew (*Ha Shem*). The English word "God" may be written as "G-d." Further, Jewish people do not say "Yahweh" or use the word "Jehovah."

It takes a full year to complete the reading of the Torah, a portion of which is read during the congregation's weekly Sabbath service. A joyous celebration (Simhat Torah) marks the completion of one year of the reading of the Torah and the beginning of readings for the next year. On this holiday, the Jewish community rejoices in God's gift of the Torah, and, holding the Torah, they sing and dance long into the night. The Torah is a symbol of God's love for the Jewish people. The wooden poles that the parchment scrolls are wound upon are called, as is the Torah itself, Tree of Life (*etz chayim*).

The study of Torah is central to the life of the Jewish community. Torah study is included in the education of Jewish children who are preparing for the ritual that will give them adult status in the congregation: *bar mitzvah* for boys, *bat mitzvah* for girls. Torah study is also part of adult education and is considered as valuable a connection to God as prayer. Just as the Talmud was built on rabbinic debate concerning observance, ritual, ethics, charity, and business practices, so does Torah study today continue, debating the meaning and application of Scripture to Jewish life in our current dynamic, evolving, worldwide community.

Lesson Plan

1. Discuss what the word "TaNaKh" means.

2. List the books in The Pentateuch/ Five Books of Moses.

3. Discuss the Torah scroll using photos and drawings. Talk about what it looks like, how it's made, where it's kept, and how it's decorated.

4. Arrange a field trip to a synagogue, and, if possible, attend a worship service where the Torah is taken from the Ark and a portion read.

5. Listen to the traditional Hebrew blessings that are said before and after a Torah reading. Discuss what they sound like and how they make the students feel.

6. Ask the students to name the Jewish people in the Torah and then in the Christian Bible. (See the introduction for a helpful list.)

7. List the descriptive phrases for God found in Hebrew prayers. Discuss the differences between this list and phrases used in Christianity.

Q&A

1. What are the Five Books of Moses?

The Pentateuch, often called the Torah, consists of the Five Books of Moses. These books are known in Christianity by English titles: Genesis, Exodus, Leviticus, Numbers, and Deuteronomy. In the Jewish community, they are known by their Hebrew titles: *B'reishit, Shemot, Vayikra, Bamidbar,* and *Devarim.*

2. How big and heavy is a Torah scroll?

A scroll that is made according to the traditional mandates can vary in height and weigh as much as twenty pounds. If stretched out, a scroll can be more than twenty-one feet long. Because of the length, a scroll that is kept rolled on two posts is opened to only the specific portion for that week and/or holiday for the reading.

3. How much does it cost to make a Torah scroll and how long does it take?

It takes many months to create a Torah and scribes usually take an entire year, writing full time, to make just one. The cost can range from $20-$60,000.

4. What is a "rabbi"?

The word "rabbi" means "teacher of the Torah." A rabbi must read and speak Hebrew, be able to read and chant from the Torah, lead the worship services, and lead the congregation in creating and maintaining Jewish communal life. Unlike priests, rabbis are encouraged to marry and have children. Traditionally, rabbis have been male. However, in the more modern branches of Judaism, it is increasingly common to see women rabbinic students and ordained rabbis.

5. Does Judaism have priests as well as rabbis?

After the destruction of the Temple in Jerusalem in 70 CE, there were no priests in Judaism. Rabbis, the teachers of the Torah, became the leaders of Jewish communities around the world.

6. What is Simhat Torah?

This holiday is on the 23rd day of the month of Tishri and follows Sukkot, the fall harvest festival. This is the celebration of completing the reading of the Torah for one year and the true beginning of a new cycle of Torah readings for the next year. Simhat Torah is Hebrew for "Rejoicing in the Torah."

TAKEAWAY PAGE

The Torah is the sacred scroll of Scripture which is divided into The Pentateuch (Five Books of Moses), the Prophets, and the Writings. The word "Torah" can be applied broadly to all of these sections as well as the rabbinic commentary on Scripture, or can refer more narrowly to The Pentateuch: Genesis, Exodus, Leviticus, Numbers, and Deuteronomy. Every week, as part of the Sabbath service, a portion of the Torah is read aloud in synagogue. The study of Torah is central to the life and worship of the Jewish community.

The prayer book for services traditionally includes Hebrew, usually with vowels for easier reading.

SUMMARY– SCRIPTURE

The Old Testament of Christianity, is known as TaNaKh in the Jewish community. This word is comprised of the Hebrew initials for Scripture's three sections: Torah, Prophets, and Writings. The term "Torah," sometimes used to describe all three sections, is the first section, the Five Books of Moses. These five books, also called The Pentateuch, are key to understanding the covenant between God and the Jewish people: Genesis, Exodus, Leviticus, Numbers, and Deuteronomy. Torah study is embedded in Jewish worship and can be widely interpreted to include the centuries of commentary in the Talmud by generations of rabbis, the teachers who are also religious leaders. While descendants of the priests of the Temple in Jerusalem still follow some of the ancient priestly rules such as not setting foot in a cemetery, it's the rabbinic laws that guide the Jewish community.

Torah scrolls are handwritten in Hebrew on sheets of parchment and are traditionally wound around two wooden poles. The Torah scroll is cherished for its history, religious significance, and artistry. It is an honor to be called to read a portion from the scroll and/or say the blessing before and after the reading during a worship service. The rabbi, as teacher and religious leader, may read the Hebrew with the ancient chants and melodies that are passed along from generation to generation.

Lesson 6: Prayer and the Sabbath

On Friday nights, Jews light candles and say the blessings for Shabbat over them, the wine, and the challah.

Introduction

The prayers, rituals, and traditions of the Sabbath are central to Judaism. The Jewish Sabbath begins at sunset on Friday and ends at sunset on Saturday. The Sabbath is a day of peace and rest. It is observed to honor God, who rested on the seventh day of creation and who brought us out of slavery to freedom. It is a time of prayer in the synagogue and of Torah study. Traditionally, the Sabbath meal is observed at home and traditions set it apart from daily life in order to keep it sacred. It's a *mitzvah*, meaning commandment, good deed, and/or blessing, to observe Shabbat, as it is pronounced in Hebrew. Christianity folded some of the elements of the Jewish Sabbath into its celebration of the Lord's Day.

Background

Preparations for the Sabbath begin during the day on Friday. The family cleans the house and themselves, preparing for the presence of God in the home. According to tradition, the Sabbath candles, not to be confused with everyday candles, are lit by the woman of the house at sunset who also says the blessings/prayers over them. The light from the candles honors the Sabbath and brings peace into the home.

On the Sabbath, the participants can glimpse the peace that is salvation. A common Sabbath greeting is "*Shabbat Shalom*," which means "Sabbath Peace." The Sabbath connects the Jewish people to God and to God's creation as described in *Genesis*. Jewish children begin learning the Sabbath prayers at a very young age and can recite them in Hebrew, giving thanks, praising God's creation, and asking for God's blessings.

The Sabbath dinner table is set with a white tablecloth, a decorative covering for the *challah* (braided bread for the Sabbath), fresh flowers, and wineglasses. The table shimmers and glows, looking like the Sabbath bride, a traditional metaphor for God's presence. The wine is blessed with a prayer, thanking God for the fruit of the vine. The prayer over the *challah* is offered as if it were the sacrifice in ancient Temple in Jerusalem and the dinner table was an altar. The bread is broken, and the pieces are shared with the family and guests who form a community around the dinner table. The meal is the biggest of the week, celebrating God's gift of nourishment and life.

Sabbath worship services in the synagogue may vary, according to the particular branch of Judaism and whether it is traditional or modern in its level of observance. Orthodox Jews may separate men and women seated in the synagogue and the service may be entirely in Hebrew.

Women will dress up and cover their heads, often with a scarf. Men will cover their heads with a hat or skullcap (*yarmulke* or *kippa*), and wear a prayer shawl *(tallit)* with traditional fringes (*tzitzit*). In the more modern branches of Judaism, both men and women may wear the *kippa* and *tallit,* but the dress usually ranges from best clothes to very informal, depending on local custom, generation, and personal preference.

At the end of the Sabbath, there is a short ceremony called "Havdalah," thanking God for creating the Sabbath and celebrating the symbols of Shabbat's end. Havdalah means "separation" and awareness of the differences between sacred time and the rest of the week. The Havdalah symbols include a spice box, a braided candle, and a cup of sweet wine. The participants pass the spice box amongst them; the tangy smell is a wakeup call for the week to come. Extinguishing of the candle into the cup of wine, after taking a sip of its sweetness, marks the end of sacred time and the beginning of the work week. Prayers and songs highlight the symbols and hopes for a good week to come.

Lesson Plan

1. Brainstorm a list of reasons why Christians pray. Identify the kind of prayers are said on the Lord's Day.

2. Discuss how Christians pray and compare that to Jewish prayer practices. Include prayer positions, places of prayer, and prayer language. (Note: Jews do not make the sign of the cross, have rosaries, go to confession, pray to Jesus, or hold their hands in prayer position. Jews do not kneel during prayer. However, some Jews may sway or gently rock back and forth during prayers.)

3. Discuss how Jewish families celebrate Shabbat in their homes on Friday nights with candles, wine, and challah.

4. Experience parts of the Jewish Sabbath either as guests at a Sabbath meal in someone's home or attended a Sabbath worship service at a synagogue.

5. Listen to traditional Sabbath songs about peace, Shalom Rav, meaning "Abundant Peace," and Sim Shalom, meaning "Grant Us Peace." Discuss how they sound and how they make you feel.

6. Watch a video of a Havdalah service and discuss what it means to the participants and the students' reaction to it.

Q&A

1. When do the Sabbath candles get blown out?

The Sabbath candles do not get blown out. They are allowed to burn out it until there is nothing left. Only the Havdalah candle is extinguished by the participants to show the end of sacred time at the conclusion of the Sabbath.

2. Are there Hebrew words used in Jewish prayers that are also used in Christian prayers?

Hebrew prayers contain some words that will be familiar to Christians including "hallelujah," "amen," and "shalom." In addition, there are phrases in Jewish prayers that will resonate with Christians, particularly phrases that begin with "bless," "blessed," and "blessings."

3. What does it mean for Jewish people to rest on the Sabbath?

The Sabbath is set aside to keep it holy. Jews are expected to reflect this holiness through contemplation, prayer, and the study of Torah. They should not go to work, or schedule a meeting for the Sabbath. The goal is to honor God's creation by resting on the seventh day, as did God. Sabbath activities center around the family and the synagogue. In more

Orthodox traditions, work is defined differently than simply going to the office and includes driving a car, traveling on a plane, and turning on the electricity.

4. Are there special foods that go along with the Sabbath meal?

The Sabbath meal includes traditional food such as the challah and wine/grape juice. There may also be food that is familiar culturally, depending on the national origin of the Jewish people at the table. For example: pickled herring and bagels and lox (smoked salmon) with cream cheese are popular dishes for Eastern European Jews. However, they have no religious significance, unlike the challah and wine.

5. When do the Jewish people go to the synagogue to pray on the Sabbath?

The timing of Sabbath services differs in the different branches of Judaism. In Orthodox Jewish congregations, Sabbath services take place on Saturday morning. Sabbath services take place on Friday night and may again occur on Saturday morning in the more modern branches.

6. What are the more modern branches of Judaism?

The modern forms of Judaism that are most well known include the Conservative, Reform, and Reconstructionist movements. They vary in their adherence to traditional interpretations of *Halakhah* (Jewish Law), the amount of Hebrew used, and tend to emphasize local and contemporary customs including *tikkun olam* (repair of the world/social justice).

TAKEAWAY PAGE

The Sabbath is the most beautiful day of the week for the Jewish people around the world. It begins at sunset on Friday and ends at sunset on Saturday. The Sabbath is a holy day, honoring God and all that God created. It is a day of rest, prayer, and Torah study. On Friday evening, Jewish families and friends share a Sabbath meal. Here are the Hebrew prayers that bless the Sabbath candles and the *challah.*

Prayer for lighting the Sabbath candles

Barukh atah Adonai, Eloheinu, melekh ha'olam

Blessed are you, Lord, our God, sovereign of the universe

asher kidishanu b'mitz'votav v'tzivanu

Who has sanctified us with His commandments and commanded us

l'had'lik neir shel Shabbat. (Amein)

to light the lights of Shabbat. (Amen)

Ha Motzi: Prayer over the bread

Barukh atah Adonai, Eloheinu, melekh ha-olam

Blessed are You, Lord, our God, King of the Universe

hamotzi lechem min ha'aretz. (Amein).

who brings forth bread from the earth. (Amen)

SUMMARY - PRAYER AND THE SABBATH

The prayers, rituals, and traditions of the Sabbath are central to Judaism. The Jewish Sabbath begins at sunset on Friday and ends at sunset on Saturday. The Sabbath is a day of peace and rest. Is observed to honor God, who rested on the seventh day of creation. It is a time of prayer in the synagogue and of Torah study. Traditionally, the Sabbath meal is observed at home and traditions set it apart from daily life in order to keep it sacred. Preparations for the Sabbath begin during the day on Friday. The family cleans the house and themselves, preparing for the presence of God in the home.

On the Sabbath, the participants can glimpse the peace that is salvation. A common Sabbath greeting is "*Shabbat Shalom*," which means "Sabbath Peace." The Sabbath dinner table is set with a white tablecloth, a decorative covering for the *challah*, (braided bread for the Sabbath), fresh flowers, and wineglasses. Jews greet the Sabbath with the same joy they'd have in greeting a bride. The meal is the biggest of the week, celebrating God's gift of nourishment and life.

Sabbath worship services in the synagogue may vary, according to the particular branch of Judaism and whether it is traditional or modern in its level of observance. At the end of the Sabbath, there is a short ceremony called "Havdalah," thanking God for creating the Sabbath and celebrating the symbols of Shabbat's end. Prayers and songs highlight the symbols and hopes for a good week to come.

Lesson 7: Gathering in the Synagogue

The synagogue's sanctuary for prayer contains the Ark with the Torah scrolls. When the Ark is opened, the congregation stands, facing the Ark, and traditionally, facing the direction of Jerusalem.

Introduction

As synagogues developed, the Jewish people established many precedents for combining tradition, ritual, prayer, and sacred space in a house of worship. History, community, and Torah intersect in this sacred space. Every synagogue has certain traditional elements that have been part of the faith for hundreds of generations, yet each synagogue also reflects the taste and character of the congregation in its architecture, seating arrangements, musicians' accommodations, and many other details. Therefore, what one experiences in the synagogue is not only a biblical people, but an evolving faith community.

Each individual Jew learns the traditions, rituals, and prayers of Judaism, but it is the communal context gives the religion much of its power. The interplay of the individual and the community is particularly visible in the celebration of the bar mitzvah (male) or the bat mitzvah (female), and in which a child is accepted into the adult congregation. This reaffirming ceremony renews the commitment of the community while it shapes the individual making the transition. This centuries-old ritual links the community to a Jewish peoplehood that transcends time and place.

Background

The Jewish community prays together in the synagogue, a word whose meaning comes from the Greek, "gather together." Some Jews refer to synagogues as temples, the reference being to the ancient Temple in Jerusalem. The Temple was built around the "Holy of Holies," where the Ark of the Covenant was kept. Built on what is now the Temple Mount of Jerusalem, the Temple was the holiest place of Judaism and is still revered today.

The Temple was destroyed in 586 BCE and again in 70 CE. During the first destruction and exile, synagogues developed as meeting places for worship, religious study, and debate. After the destruction of the second Temple, the synagogue became the focus of Judaism and continues to be the house of worship for contemporary Jewish communities throughout the world.

The rituals, altar, and sacrifices of the Temple were replaced by prayers and traditions in the synagogue at home. The synagogue became a place of prayer, study, and of rabbis rather than priests. Traditionally, the legacy of the Temple is honored by facing the direction of Jerusalem during prayer. Since the destruction of the second Temple, the rabbinic laws and commentary in the Talmud have guided the Jewish community. The Torah scrolls became the center of worship and of the synagogue itself.

The scrolls are kept in a structure called the *Aron HaKodesh*, which translates as the "Holy Vestibule." Colloquially known as The Ark, it can be very simple or quite ornate, depending on the congregation. Over the Ark is a continually burning light, the *Ner Tamid* (Eternal Light), which best symbolizes the eternal covenant of God with the Jewish people. The Ark and the *Ner Tamid* are often elevated so that the entire congregation can see them and know that they are part of the centuries-long tradition.

The congregants may sit during much of the service, but they stand in respect when the Ark is opened and the Torah scrolls are visible. It is an honor to be called up to read from the Torah or recite the Hebrew prayers before and after the Torah portion. The *siddur* (prayer book) guides the congregation through the service.

In a tradition that has carried over into Christianity, Jewish worship begins with praise, blessings, and a call to worship with phrases such as "Blessed are you, Lord our God," and "Praised be you, Almighty God." While English translations of the Hebrew, especially in the modern branches of Judaism, Hebrew remains the sacred language of Jewish prayer. The Hebrew prayer called The *Shema* is central to the Jewish religion and often called the watchword of the faith. The *Shema* calls upon Jews to declare God's eternal and supreme name and to renew their covenant with God through demonstrations of love and respect. The complete *Shema* includes related prayers and verses from, among other scriptural sources, *Deuteronomy* 6:4 - 9 and 11:13 - 21, but is best known as, "Hear O Israel: the Lord our God, the Lord is One!" (*Deuteronomy* 6:4).

The importance of passing down tradition from generation to generation is easily seen in the rituals of the bar/bat mitzvah. This is the ceremony where boys and girls gain adult privileges and responsibilities at age thirteen, although conservative Jewish girls may do this at age twelve, and traditional Jewish girls may not participate. This study of Hebrew, history, holidays, prayers, and especially the Torah is required for the ceremony. The Torah is handed for members of the oldest generation to the child, who in addition to being called to read the Torah for the first time, must also make a speech demonstrating readiness for the new role. In this way, the dynamics of individual and communal life are renewed within the synagogue.

Lesson Plan

1. Using the photographs in this book, explore the synagogue. What do you see that reminds you of the Christian church? What do you see this is different? Name and point out important features of the synagogue: Torah scroll, the bimah, the Ark, the Eternal Light.

2. Discuss the *Shema* prayer and listen to it in Hebrew. What does it mean to the Jewish people? What are some of the central prayers of Christianity? How are they different and how are they similar?

3. Discuss the bar mitzvahs that students may have seen on television, at the movies, or attended. Talk about it meaning in the life of a young Jewish person.

4. Arrange to visit a synagogue and make a list of everything visual about the experience. Discuss what was seen on the field trip. Research anything that was not understood.

5. Assign a similar visual experience for the church and increase awareness of the visual elements of religious tradition.

Q&A

1. Why don't Christians use Hebrew in their worship services?

While there are a few Hebrew words in the Christian liturgy, Christianity developed using translations of the Bible from the Greek and Latin.

2. Where is the altar for the sacrifices described in the Hebrew Scriptures?

There is no altar synagogues because there are no sacrifices of grains, fruits, or animals. Those sacrifices were made by the priests in the Temple of Jerusalem and at no other time or place in Judaism.

3. What are the ways in which the Jewish people do remember that temple in Jerusalem?

While the rituals of the Temple have been replaced by prayer, Jewish congregations face Jerusalem during prayer, honoring their legacy. In addition, at every Jewish wedding, the bridegroom crushes a glass with his foot. The breaking of the glass symbolizes the destruction of the second Temple in Jerusalem, but it is also a reminder of the faith that has carried Jews through past generations and that will continue to carry them into the future.

4. How do you open the Ark to take out one of the Torah scrolls?

The Ark usually has two doors that meet in the middle. Each door is slid open to the outer side by a member of the congregation, all of whom stand in respect. The Torah scrolls rest inside until the worship leader removes and "undresses" its bells, breastplate, and covering. The congregation is seated when the Torah is opened, prayers are chanted, and a portion of the Torah is read.

TAKEAWAY PAGE

While honoring the ancient Temple in Jerusalem, the synagogue is a place of prayer, study, and gathering for Jewish communities around the world. The Torah scrolls are kept in the Ark, above which the *Ner Tamid* is constantly lit, symbolizing God's eternal light. The sacred language of prayer is Hebrew is central to the Jewish religion as is *The Shema* (and related set of prayers) which is often called the watchword of the faith. The study of Hebrew and the prayers in the Torah are required for the ritual of the child entering into the adult congregation. The bar/bat mitzvah ceremony takes place in the synagogue, passing down tradition, and Jewish observance from one generation to the next, and the next, and to the generations to come.

שְׁמַע יִשְׂרָאֵל יְיָ אֱלֹהֵינוּ יְיָ אֶחָד

The Shema

Sh'ma Yisrael Adonai Eloheinu Adonai Eḥad

"Hear, O Israel: the Lord our God, the Lord is one."

OR

"Hear, O Israel: The Lord is our God, the Lord alone."

SUMMARY- GATHERING IN THE SYNAGOGUE

As synagogues developed, the Jewish people established many precedents for combining tradition, ritual, prayer, and sacred space in a house of worship. History, community, and Torah intersect in this sacred space. Every synagogue has elements that represent the traditions of hundreds of generations. Yet, each synagogue also reflects the taste and character of the congregation in its architecture, seating arrangements, musicians' accommodations, and many other details. Each individual Jew learns the traditions, rituals, and prayers of Judaism, but it is the communal context that gives the religion much of its power. The interplay of the individual and the community is particularly visible in the celebration of the bar mitzvah (male) or the bat mitzvah (female), in which a child is accepted into the adult congregation. This reaffirming ceremony renews the commitment of the community while it shapes the individual making the transition. This centuries-old ritual links the community to a Jewish peoplehood that transcends time and place.

Jewish communities pray together in synagogues around the world. Some Jews refer to synagogues as temples, the reference being to the ancient Temple in Jerusalem. The Temple was built around the "Holy of Holies," where the Ark of the Covenant was kept. Built on the Temple Mount of Jerusalem, the Temple was the holiest place of Judaism and is still revered today.

The Temple was destroyed in 586 BCE and again in 70 CE. After the fall of the second Temple, the synagogue became the focus of Judaism and continues to be the house of worship for contemporary Jewish communities throughout the world.

The rituals, altar, and sacrifices of the Temple were replaced by prayers and traditions. The synagogue became a place for prayer, study, and gathering together, the original meaning of this Greek word. The legacy of the Temple is honored by facing the direction of Jerusalem during prayer. The Torah scrolls became the center of worship and of the synagogue itself. The scrolls are kept in a structure called the Ark, which can be very simple or quite ornate, depending on the congregation. Over the Ark is a continually burning light, the *Ner Tamid* (Eternal Light) best symbolizes the eternal covenant of God with the Jewish people. The Ark and the *Ner Tamid* are often elevated so that the entire congregation can see them and know that they are part of the centuries-long tradition.

The importance of passing down tradition from generation to generation is easily seen in the rituals of the bar/bat mitzvah, the ceremony where children gain adult privileges and responsibilities at age thirteen. The Torah is handed from members of the oldest generation to the child, who in addition to being called to read the Torah for the first time, must also make a speech demonstrating readiness for the new role. In this way, the dynamics of individual and communal life are renewed within the synagogue.

APPENDIX A: JEWISH SACRED FOOD

Note on pronunciation:

The English equivalent of Hebrew words are approximations and you may see varying spellings. A major reason for discrepancies between Hebrew and English is the presence of sounds in the Hebrew alphabet that have no English equivalent. It is recommended that where one sees the guttural-sounding "ch," that it is generally pronounced as an "k," given the unfamiliarity with the Hebrew sound. There are also variations in pronunciation within Judaism itself. The pronunciation in this book is Sephardic, which means that the preferred ending of many words will be "t" rather than "s" (e.g. bat mitzvah rather than bas mitzvah).

Few issues generate as many practical questions about Judaism as the role of food. "What to serve?", "What not to serve?", and "How to prepare?" are frequent concerns when trying to show respect and respond to the needs of Jewish friends, students, and colleagues. The answers to these questions may vary, depending on how traditional or modern the branch of Judaism and how strictly the individual follows the Kashrut laws for what food is permitted and is considered kosher. With thousands of years of decisions on what is kosher, kosher food is part of Jewish identity around the globe, even as there are cultural, national, and personal differences. While it is not possible to provide all details of this complex topic, this introduction will cover major issues with the understanding that assumptions should be avoided. If in doubt, demonstrate respect and good intentions by asking about food choices.

Kashrut laws forbid mixing milk and meat based on the biblical verse, "Do not cook a kid in its mother's milk." which appears in *Exodus* and *Deuteronomy*. Many traditional Jews will only eat food with a kosher label to guarantee the kosher manufacturing of all ingredients. Further, only certain animals (both on land and at sea) are permitted for consumption. Pork and shellfish are forbidden and meat from cows, while permitted, must be slaughtered correctly.

For many Jewish people, a vegetarian meal is acceptable. The meal must contain only neutral items called parve or pareve (Yiddish), meaning food that is neither meat nor dairy. However, vegetables may need to be served on paper plates and with plastic/disposable utensils for more traditional Jews who maintain separate plates for milk and meat in their homes. Understand that some Jewish guests or students may choose not to eat anything at your table, may require a pre-packaged kosher meal, or may ask to bring their own food.

Quick Kosher Guide

QUICK KOSHER GUIDE			
Kashrut Labels	Non-Kosher ("*Treif*")	Major Fasts	Preparation
Kosher symbols certify: Supervised production Inspected facilities Examined ingredients Identify the rabbinic agency and certification Designated category of use: • Meat only • Dairy only • Neutral/Pareve • Passover	Taboo Meat: Kosher animals must have cloven hoof, chew cud/grass, (No pork) Kosher slaughter (No bloody meat, certified) Taboo Dairy: No non-kosher animals No non-kosher ingredients/additives Must be certified as kosher Cannot be from a non-kosher animal. Cannot have ingredients that are meat derivatives: hard cheese made with rennet, yogurt that contains gelatin, and butter with non-kosher additives. Must be processed on kosher equipment. Taboo Seafood: No shellfish Kosher fish must have fins & scales. (No catfish, shark, eels, swordfish) No sea mammals (No whales, dolphins) Misc. Ingredients: No gelatin, dyes, or additives from treif -related products	Yom Kippur: 10th day of the month of Tishri - Day of Atonement Tishah B'Av: 9th day of the month of Av - destruction of the Temple/Jerusalem Passover: Partial Fast - no leavening	Glatt Kosher: Stricter standards for defect-free, kosher meat Kosher for Passover: No "chametz" grains: wheat, barley, rye, spelt or oats (unless specially prepared with rabbinic supervision to prevent leavening) Meat: All animals, fowl, and their byproducts, such as bones, soup, or gravy are considered meat Dairy: All foods from or containing milk are considered dairy: milk, butter, yogurt, and all cheese "Pareve" - Neutral Food that is neither meat nor diary, don't have these ingredients, or are prepared/cooked with them Includes unprocessed vegetables, fruits, eggs, fish, grains as well as coffee, tea, soft drinks and some candy/snacks if labeled "pareve"

APPENDIX B: MORE ON HOLIDAYS

The Jewish "day" begins and ends at sunset, rather than at midnight and that's when holidays begin. Work is not permitted on Rosh Hashanah, on Yom Kippur, on the first and second days of Sukkot, on Shemini Atzeret, on Simchat Torah, on Shavu'ot, and the first, second, seventh and eighth days of Passover. The "work" prohibited on those holidays is the same as traditionally prohibited on Shabbat, except that cooking, baking, transferring fire and carrying are permitted.

Celebrating an extra day on some holidays originated during a time when lunar calendars were difficult to obtain as were precise dates of observance. It's not a custom maintained by Israelis, but has been adopted by traditional Jews elsewhere, for example, on Rosh Hashanah.

There are other holidays that shape the Jewish calendar besides those already featured in this book: Shabbat, Rosh Hashanah, Yom Kippur, Sukkot, Hanukkah, Pesach (Passover), and Shavu'ot. Here are some widely celebrated holidays:

Shemini Atzeret & Simchat Torah: Shemini Atzeret is a joyous after-gathering to the seven days of Sukkot. In Israel, Shemini Atzeret is also the holiday of Simchat Torah. Elsewhere, Shemini Atzeret lasts two days and the second day is Simchat Torah (month of Tishri 22 and 23).

Simchat Torah ("Rejoicing in the Torah") marks the completion of the annual cycle of weekly Torah readings. The holiday is observed by reading the last chapter in Deuteronomy and immediately proceeding to the first chapter of Genesis, creating a never-ending cycle. Simchat Torah is celebrated by processions around the synagogue carrying Torah scrolls.

Tu B'Shevat: A holiday known as the New Year for Trees. Tu (the number 15) B'Shevat literally means the 15th day of the Jewish month of Shevat. The holiday is not mentioned in the Torah but is commonly observed by planting trees, or raising funds to plant trees in Israel.

Purim: A joyous and carnival-like holiday with costumes, contests, noise makers, and tasty treats. It celebrates Jews being saved from destruction in ancient Persia, and, by extension, saved from destruction in modern times. The Purim story is told in the Biblical book of Esther who was a beautiful young woman living in Persia, raised by her cousin Mordecai. Esther was sent to the harem of Persia's King Ahasuerus who made her queen, not knowing she was Jewish.

The villain of the story is Haman, an advisor to King Ahasuerus. Mordecai refused to bow down to Haman who then plotted to destroy the Jewish people. Mordecai persuaded Esther to speak to the king on behalf of the Jewish people, a dangerous action when not summoned by the king to speak. In the end, the Jewish people were saved, and Haman was destroyed. The word "Purim" means "lots" and refers to the lottery used by Haman to choose the date for the massacre, the 13th of Adar. Purim is celebrated a day later on the 14th day of Adar.

Lag b'Omer: The Counting of the Omer connects Pesach (Exodus) to Shavu'ot (giving of the Torah) by counting and praying every night from the second night of Passover to the night before Shavu'ot. The forty days of partial mourning with no weddings or formal celebrations, is a reminder that redemption from slavery was only completed when the Torah was received. The exception to this period of mourning is the thirty-third day, which is Lag b'Omer.

MODERN HOLIDAYS - POST-WORLD WAR II

Holocaust Remembrance Day: The Day (27th day of the month of Nissan) honors all who died in the Holocaust. It commemorates the anniversary of the Warsaw ghetto uprising where Polish Jews fought against extermination and deportation to death camps during World War II. The term for Holocaust in Hebrew is "Shoah." Holocaust Remembrance Day is called Yom Hashoah. The United States official memorial, the Holocaust Memorial Museum (USHMM), is next to the Washington, D.C. National Mall. The USHMM provides documentation, study, and interpretation of Holocaust history. Since opening in 1993, it's helped citizens of the world confront hatred, prevent genocide, and promote human dignity.

Yom Ha'atzmaut: Independence Day commemorates the 1948 declaration establishing the State of Israel by Jewish leadership led by future Prime Minister David Ben-Gurion. Celebrated on the 5th day of the month of Iyar, Yom Ha'atzmaut is preceded by Yom Hazikaron, the Israeli Fallen Soldiers and Victims of Terrorism Remembrance Day.

APPENDIX C: COLORING PAGES

The Sukkah

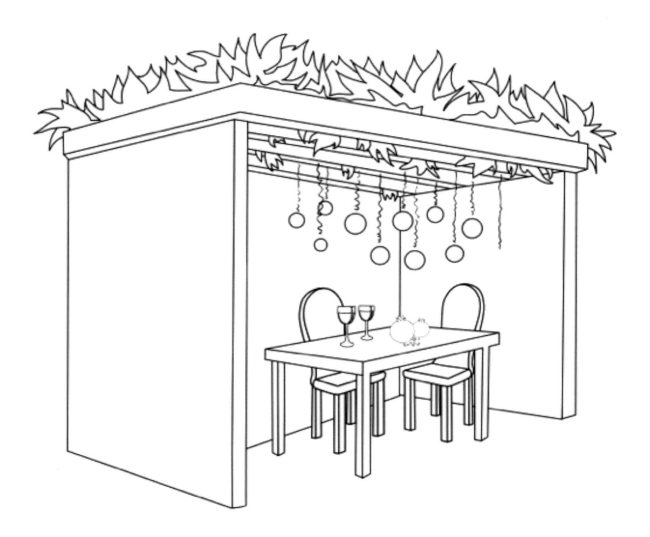

Share this coloring page of a Sukkah in which Jews celebrate the harvest festival of Sukkot.

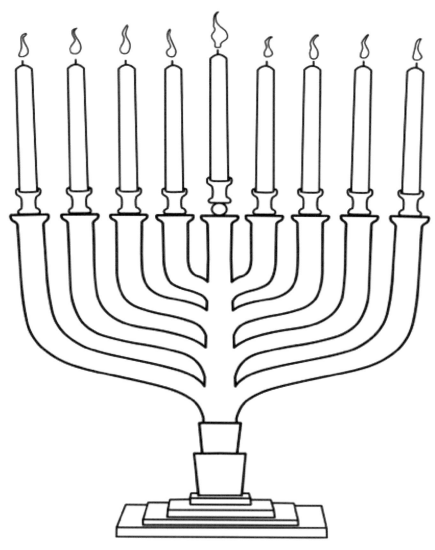

Share this coloring page of a Hanukkah menorah used for candle lighting each night during the holiday of Hanukkah.

APPENDIX D: GLOSSARY

Ark: Cabinet that houses the Torah scrolls, often built into the wall of the synagogue. Often decorative and visually central, the Ark is the visual focus of the synagogue, symbolizing the original Ark of the Covenant.

B.C.E.: Abbreviation for the phrase "Before the Common Era." This is the terminology used in the Jewish community rather than B.C. ("Before Christ"), which is not a frame of reference in Judaism. The abbreviation C. E. is also interpreted as the "Common Era," which is used in place of A. D. - *Anno Domini* in Latin.

Bar Mitzvah: The celebration marking a Jewish boy's attainment of adult status in the congregation. It is usually celebrated at age thirteen and requires the boy to read from the Torah in front of the congregation.

Bat Mitzvah: The celebration marking a Jewish girl's attainment of adult status in the congregation. It is celebrated in the more modern Jewish branches: Reform, Reconstructionist, and some Conservative synagogues.

Bima: Originally from the Greek meaning "raised platform." The bima is a raised area from which worship services are often led.

B'reshit: From the Hebrew meaning "In the beginning," The opening phrase of the *Book of Genesis*.

Challah: Braided bread baked specifically for the Sabbath.

Charoset: Traditional combination of chopped apples, nuts, cinnamon, and red wine (Ashkenazic version). It is eaten at Passover and symbolizes the mortar of the bricks that the slaves had to make.

Conservative Judaism: Branch of Judaism that blends tradition with modern practices.

Dayenu: Sixth-century song of joy and thanksgiving sung during the Passover Seder meal. In Hebrew the word means "that would have been enough" and refers to each of God's miracles while bringing the Israelites out of Egypt to Mount Sinai and to the Promised Land.

Days of Awe: The ten High Holy Days counting from Rosh HaShanah (New Year) to Yom Kippur (Day of Atonement).

Dreidel: Spinning top traditionally associated with Hanukkah.

The Four Questions: The ritual questions that are part of the Passover liturgy. They define sacred aspects of the Passover Seder and encouraging the retelling of the story of Exodus from Egypt.

Gelt: From the Yiddish, meaning "money," often referring to gifts of money during Hanukkah. In modern times, Hanukkah gelt is also refers to gold foil-wrapped chocolate candy in the shape of coins.

Haggadah: Passover book that gives the order of the Seder service, the readings, the prayers, and the songs.

Hanukkah: Festival of Lights celebrating the rededication of the ancient Temple in Jerusalem.

Ha Shem: From the Hebrew meaning "the name." It refers to the name of God, which is sacred and not allowed to be said or written in the Jewish tradition.

Hassidim: Ultra-Orthodox group within Judaism of Eastern European origin that adheres to Yiddish (Combination of Hebrew, German & Eastern European) tradition and often characterized by a modest style of dress.

Havdalah: Brief ceremony closing the Sabbath and beginning the week. The literal meaning is "separation."

Holocaust: Also known as The Shoah, the Holocaust refers to historical events of World War II when six million Jews, one third of the world's Jewish population, were systematically killed by the Nazi regime.

Kol Nidre: One of the most solemn prayers in Judaism. The prayer and its music is identified with Yom Kippur.

Kosher: Refers to the dietary laws of Judaism. Food that is kosher is often given the approval of rabbinic organizations designed for this purpose.

Latkes: Potato pancakes traditionally linked to Hanukkah celebrations.

Maccabees: From the Hebrew meaning "hammer," referring to a small group of Jews, led by Judah Maccabee, who held against foreign domination and religious oppression in the second century BCE. The Hanukkah story is the story of the Maccabees battle to regain the Temple in Jerusalem and the rededication of the Temple after its desecration.

Matzoh: Unleavened bread eaten during Passover according to the dietary laws of those holy days.

Menorah: The 7-branch candelabrum in the synagogue. The Hanukkah menorah, the hannukiyah, is 9-branch candelabrum with its ninth candle used for lighting the other eight.

Mezzuzah: Small casing containing a piece of parchment inscribed with verses from Dueteronomy that include the commandment to write God's words on the doorpost of one's house. The Mezzuzah is a valued possession, often beautifully and artistically fashioned, that is fixed to the doorpost, affirming the sanctity of the Jewish home.

Mitzvah: From the Hebrew meaning "good deed, blessing, and commandment" combined.

Mogen David: From the Hebrew meaning "Shield of David" referring to the six-pointed star. Since the Middle Ages, the Jewish Star has been a symbol of the Jewish people.

Ne'er Tamid: From the Hebrew referring to the eternal light symbolizing the covenant between God and the Jewish people. The Ne'er Tamid is continuously lit and placed in front/above the Ark in the synagogue.

Orthodox Judaism: Branch of Judaism that emphasizes traditional celebrations and interpretation of Hebrew Scripture.

Pesach: From the Hebrew commonly translated as "Passover," referring to the spring harvest/pilgrimage holiday and commemoration of the Exodus from Egypt.

Rabbi: From the Hebrew meaning "teacher," often referring to the chief religious official of a synagogue, who is usually trained, educated, and ordained.

Reconstructionist Judaism: Branch of Judaism that originated from Conservative Judaism, but emphasizes certain modern themes, particularly the importance of a Jewish peoplehood.

Reform Judaism: Branch of Judaism that has led the movement to adapt the religion to modern times, particularly prominent in the United States.

Rosh HaShanah: From the Hebrew meaning "Head of the Year," referring to the Jewish New Year.

Seder: From the Hebrew meaning "Order." It refers to the rituals of the Passover meal.

Shabbat: The Jewish Sabbath, beginning at sunset on Friday and continuing until sunset on Saturday. Often heard in the phrase, "Shabbat Shalom," a common greeting that offers "Sabbath Peace."

Shavuot: Summer harvest/ pilgrimage festival associated with Moses receiving the Ten Commandments.

Sh'ma Yisrael: The first two words of the Hebrew prayer often known as the "*Shema*" that is the centerpiece of the Jewish prayer service. The prayer underscores both the monotheism and the covenant between God and the Jewish people that are central to Judaism.

Shofar: Ram's horn blown as part of the worship service on Rosh Hashanah and again at the closing of the Ten Days of Awe at the end of Yom Kippur.

Simchat Torah: From the Hebrew meaning "Rejoicing in the Torah," referring to the celebration each year of completing the reading of the Torah and beginning it anew.

Sukkot: From the Hebrew meaning "Booths," referring to the Fall harvest/ pilgrimage festival giving thanks for God's bounty. A Booth, called a "sukkah," is a temporary dwelling of four sides and a flat roof echoing biblical times when Jews stayed in similar booths in their fields during the time of harvest.

Synagogue: Jewish house of worship, sometimes referred to as a "temple," echoing a sense of the ancient Temple in Jerusalem.

Talmud: Rabbinic laws and commentary on the Hebrew Scriptures extended over generations and centuries. While often referred to as the Jewish oral tradition, the rabbinic debates and decisions are contained in two compiled books, The Mishnah and The Gemara. The Talmud is central to understanding Judaism.

Tanakh: Acronym for The Hebrew Scriptures with letters symbolizing the three sections: Torah (The Five Books of Moses), Nevi'im (The Prophets), and Kethuvim (The Writings). The term "Torah" is often used to refer to all three sections of Hebrew Scriptures, and is used by some to also include the Talmud commentaries.

Yiddish: A language spoken by many Jewish people combining Hebrew, German & Eastern European languages in a unique, distinctive cultural dialect. Common to Jewish immigrants who came in historic waves to the United States from Europe, Yiddish phrases have seeped into American slang.

About the Author

Deborah J. Levine is an award-winning author, Editor-in-Chief of the American Diversity Report, and a blogger for The Huffington Post. She is trainer specializing in cross-cultural communication and religious diversity.

Deborah is a(n) . . .

. . . Cross-Cultural Consultant: Deborah trains corporations, nonprofits, education institutions, and government agencies on Diversity & Inclusion using storytelling strategies. She created Chattanooga's Community Global Leadership Class and was chief consultant for Chattanooga's Teen Global Leadership Class.

. . . . Award-winning Author: Her articles appeared in *The American Journal of Community Psychology, The Journal of Public Management & Social Policy, Harvard Divinity School Bulletin, The Bermudian Magazine* and *The Christian Century.* She served as Research Coordinator at the College of Engineering and Computer Science /U. of TN at Chattanooga (UTC).

. . . Civic Leader: She served on the Volkswagen Chattanooga Diversity Task Force and the boards of Society of Diversity Professionals & Executives, Association of Trainers & Developers/ATD, and National Association of Women Business Owners/NAWBO. Deborah founded the Women's Council on Diversity/ Women GroundBreakers, and the DuPage Interfaith Resource Network. She is the recipient of awards from the National Catholic Press Association, American Planning Association/Chicago, TN Economic Council on Women, and Girls Inc./Chattanooga.

. . . Education: Deborah has undergraduate coursework in cultural anthropology (Harvard University, BS-New York University) and a Master's degree in Urban Planning & Policy (MUPP-U. of Illinois/Chicago) which she designed/pioneered in cultural planning. Deborah has a Master's degree in religion (MJS-Spertus Institute) and several research fellowships (Hebrew Union College, UCLA).

Made in the USA
Columbia, SC
22 August 2024

40809144R00044